The Last "Motivational" Book You'll Ever Need

The Indestructible Formula to Be Unstoppable and Achieve Your Goals

By Mark Erdat

Copyright Mark Erdat © 2020

All rights reserved. No part of this publication may be reproduced, stored in a retrieval system, or transmitted, in any form or by any means, electronic, mechanical, photocopying, recording or otherwise, without the prior written permission of the author and the publishers.

The scanning, uploading, and distribution of this book via the Internet or via any other means without the permission of the author are illegal and punishable by law. Please purchase only authorized electronic editions, and do not participate in or encourage electronic piracy of copyrighted materials.

Disclaimer

All information in this book has been carefully researched and checked for factual accuracy. However, the author and publishers make no warranty, expressed or implied, that the information contained herein is appropriate for every individual, situation, or purpose, and assume no responsibility for errors or omission. The reader assumes the risk and full responsibility for all actions, and the author will not be held liable for any loss or damage, whether consequential, incidental and special or otherwise, that may result from the information presented in this publication.

The information presented in this book is not meant to substitute any professional, medical, or legal advice. Readers are advised to consult qualified professionals regarding any specific legal, medical, financial, or mental health advice.

This book is for inspirational and entertainment purposes only.

Contents

Ready to Be Unstoppable?.......................................5

Introduction and the Bold Promise.......................8

Step #1 Realize Why You Don't Achieve Your Goals in the Desired Timeline 22

Step #2 Why Waiting for Unlimited Motivation Can Be a Trap and What You Should Focus on Instead 42

Step #3 What Most Motivational Books Miss—Your Commitment Muscle 54

Step #4 Your No-Complaint Muscle 74

Final Words—The 10 Commandments of the Unstoppable Achiever 84

Ready to Be Unstoppable?

Warning! If you're looking for another superficial "motivational book" because you hope to get motivated without working on yourself, then this book is not for you! This book is not designed for passive reading while hoping for a miracle. And it's definitely not for the faint of heart or those desperate for a magic motivational pill!

However, if you're ready to shift your mindset, do the inner work, and follow a proven formula to actually achieve your goals (even if you've failed before), you've come to the right place!

Whether you want to transform your body, succeed in your career/business, radically improve your discipline, or eradicate bad habits, this book will give you answers and a proven, step-by-step blueprint to follow.

Only for ambitious and serious people who are ready to make changes in their lives!

The Last Motivational Book You'll Ever Need focuses on the missing factors to help you stay motivated to achieve your goals, even if things don't go as planned.

Here's exactly what you're going to learn:

- Why most people don't actually struggle with motivation (even though they think they do), what the main problem is, and how to fix it
- The biggest motivational myths and why they do more harm than good
- The hidden force stopping you from achieving your goals faster and a simple exercise to make it work in your favor
- Simple mindset shifts that will make you unstoppable, even if you feel like crap
- Why failure can be your best friend and motivator
- The shocking truth behind the motivational self-help industry (and how to use it for your advantage!)
- How to figure out if you're working toward the right goals
- The hidden dangers of most "motivational books" out there and how to protect your mind
- Exactly how to use fear to your advantage and be unstoppable

Life is too short to waste on things that don't get you closer to your goals.

If you're sick and tired of ivory-tower gurus, fake positivity, and outdated information that doesn't work in real life, and are ready to transform your life forever, keep reading, because it looks like you've found the right book to guide you.

Introduction and the Bold Promise

Dear reader, thank you so much for taking an interest in this book. And yes, I can pretty much guess what's going on in your head right now. Perhaps you're curious; after all, the title says this could be the last "motivational" book you'll ever need to read.

Maybe you even feel a bit scared, because you already know this book is not designed for passive reading and you will be asked to do some work as you're reading this book.

Even though this could be the last motivational book you'll ever need, it's designed to be read multiple times. So, whenever you feel like your mindset slips back, be sure to re-read it and do the exercises from this book.

So, how is my book different from other self-help or motivational books you may have read in the past?

Now, I don't want to sound condescending or like someone who knows it all. I'm not a guru, and if anything, I'm anti-guru, anti-cult, and anti-cookie-cutter self-help. My biggest personal goal in life is to be myself as much as I can. If you ever asked me for a number-one piece of advice for motivation and anything else in life, I'd tell you to dive deep first and figure out who you truly are. Authenticity is your best friend! More on that later.

When it comes to books on the topic of motivation or self-development, there are two kinds of them:

The first category:

There is this "feel good, just think positive, read this book and your life will change, I'll gently hold your hand" kind of book.

The second category:

"You're lazy; you're a loser, it's time to take massive action and do something right here, right now!!!"

In both cases, some authors who write those books write pretty much about themselves, as if it was some kind of biography. Or they even look down on you and try to distract you with some fluff.

Although this is not always the case, as someone who's read hundreds of self-help books, this is the case for most of them.

Now, personally, I feel like there is some value in both "feel good, gentle, and fluffy motivational books", as well as more aggressive "just get over yourself, you loser, I'll kick your ass" motivational books.

The first one may be good to fill your mind with positivity, especially when you're going through some rough patches. The second kind of books works well if you really need a push to do something because you've been lazy. The first one may be good if you're rebuilding yourself after experiencing some problems or traumas, and the second one is great to help you get out of the victim mindset.

So, I'm not discrediting any of those kinds of books. The problem is when people read the first kind (the overly feel-good books), and never take any action.

Yes, positive thinking is great if backed up by positive action. And most people skip the action part!

Yes, those feel-good books may offer some insights to focus on the positive, and may even help you on your self-development and spiritual journey. But, ultimately, if there is no action, there's nothing. Many people keep looking for more and more positive and "motivational" stuff. Even if they feel motivated for a short period of time, they never do anything, and the feeling of temporary excitement goes away. In other words, the mere feeling of being motivated will not lead to success if a person doesn't take action.

Now, the second kind of a motivational book or material is more aggressive, and the author keeps calling you out on your BS.

And like I said, there's some value in it for a specific kind of person and in some situations. Yes, it can give you a push so that you get over yourself and take action.

The danger is that you may end up arrogant, cynical, and looking down on everyone. You may also end up burnt out. Or you may proceed to take mindless action, without any vision. Thus, accomplishing specific goals that make you happy can get harder and harder.

The problem with many self-development books is that they're not practical and don't offer specific steps to follow.

Some may do, but on the backend, so you pay for a book, feel all pumped up, and then read the book, only to find out that all your answers are just a few thousand dollars away if you purchase some expensive course or seminar.

This is why I decided to create a short book that fuses all the good stuff, from both feel-good, "get to know yourself" stuff as well as the "take massive action, get over yourself, and stop whining" kind of books.

Not only that, but I also designed my own system to help you get clear on what you really want, what is stopping you, and how to figure out the steps to help you stay not only motivated but also committed, so that you can keep going even if things get tough.

To make one thing clear and be 100% transparent- the system I share in this book comes from my own experience as a business owner and self-development enthusiast. I'm not a scientist, and this book is not about the latest research on human psychology, but is instead a practical guide written by a simple guy who wanted to give back.

I didn't write this book to get you to my funnels or other projects. In fact, I keep my writing separate from all my businesses, and it's not my attempt to convert my readers into clients. I want to keep it simple, transparent, and easy to follow. This book is all you need.

Well, almost all you need, because you will also need a notebook to go through this book, and I highly recommend you avoid passive reading. Chances are you've already done enough passive reading in the past. Now is the best time to change your life!

So, go through this book at your own pace, but for God's sake, do the exercises I recommend you do.

Now, I may sound a bit like a guru, or some online marketer with a "new, cutting-edge system."

Which is not my intention at all.

Feel free to do the exercises your own way; after all, everyone is different. There is no right or wrong way of doing them. Just do them, and your life will start to get better and better!

While I can't promise you an instant six-pack or a million dollars after reading this book (or even after doing the exercises), I feel positive that you will drastically improve your life and achieve a state of peace and inner liberation that will allow you to pursue your goals with conviction and confidence.

Also, I don't want to sound unsympathetic, but this book can't help a lifelong excuse maker or complainer. And it's not something that you can just passively read to magically feel motivated so that you can finally change your life. First, you need to sort yourself out!

I see this complaint all the time! People read motivational books, expecting the author to make them feel motivated and reach a certain state, so that they don't even have to feel responsible for any changes in their lives and perhaps even blame the book and the authors.

Well, it doesn't work that way!

Now, if you're reading this, I'm pretty sure you're laughing because you're a high achiever, and you know that the last paragraph wasn't about you.

But, I'll make a bold statement and say this:

We all have something from the victim and blaming mindset. And it's a lifelong journey to keep eliminating all those weeds: lack of responsibility and victimhood. It's easy to blame someone else's weeds, right? And I'm here with you, and I'll be the first one to admit I'm not perfect, and every single day I find myself getting rid of more and more weeds!

At the same time, never think you're better than someone else, because your mindset is better. It's a mistake I made in the past, and it didn't serve me very well because I thought I was so good and successful, I stopped learning.

And we should never stop learning. It's a lifelong journey!

You're not better than other people and you're not worse than other people. If you ever find yourself feeling unworthy or comparing yourself to other people, promise yourself to become aware of it and release it too (this book will be offering some practical steps on how to get rid of all those weeds by shifting your identity).

To sum up: victim mindset, blaming others, resentment, lack of responsibility, and feeling superior or inferior are all the biggest motivation and high-performance killers.

Think about it. What was the last thing or project that didn't go that well? Who did you blame- your spouse, the government, or maybe the client who canceled the contract?

At the same time, I don't want you to feel bad. I just want you to become aware of negative patterns in your life so you can prevent certain circumstances from happening again.

You don't have it so bad, and the world is not out to get you. You're not the center of the world, and not everyone is looking at you or thinking about you.

The bottom line is that someone always has it better than you or worse than you. Some people were born richer and some poorer. So what?

Your situation is different and unique in a good way, so never compare yourself to other people. Don't compare yourself to others to feel superior or inferior. Just embrace who you are, what you have been through, and what resources you have available to you right here, right now. Embrace your mistakes and wins. Embrace what you like and don't like about yourself. Just let it be.

Now, as I said in the beginning, some authors write "motivational" books where 99% of the book is about themselves and reads like a biography. Nothing against biographies - there is a lot of value in them. But I always appreciate if a book is in the right category, to know what I'm getting into!

I guess that most people who read any kind of self-development book are looking for practical information they can use to improve their lives. They are not necessarily interested in reading three hundred pages about the author's successes.

So, in alignment with that, I'm focusing on you and the tools that can help you, not on how cool I am (although, you gotta admit I am pretty cool for writing this book). However, you may be wondering how I came up with all this, so here's a little bit about myself and my story.

I used to be homeless, even though I was born in a pretty good family. Not rich, but a decent, lower-middle-class family where we had food, clothes, and all the basic stuff we needed. I made some wrong choices in my life, and for a few months, I was homeless.

I take all responsibility for that, even though my family was a bit toxic and I could blame them if I wanted. However, I only blame myself and my own life for what happened.

But here's the thing. Being homeless and hitting rock bottom made me self-reflect, and it was how I got into self-development. At first, I wanted to figure out why people I grew up with, coming from a similar background, made something out of themselves while I ended up homeless.

Eventually, I realized that everything happened *for* me, not *to* me. During the few months of being homeless, I learned a lot about myself and to appreciate all the small things in life.

I decided to improve myself; I changed my attitude and my mindset. One thing I realized is that we always have a choice! Some people end up on the streets and still have pride and dignity, and choose to improve their situation. And others choose to drink or even do drugs to forget, and their attitude is *it all happened to me, nobody wants to help me,* or *the council or the government doesn't care.*

Now, I know this sounds very harsh, but I have been there too. And trust me when I say this: I met people who were in a much worse situation than me, and now they're way more successful than me.

It all comes down to your mindset, choices, responsibility, and your personal dignity.

Likewise, I met people who were born rich in very good and influential families with many resources, yet their levels of happiness, success, and fulfillment are now much lower than someone who was living on the streets and simply chose to make something of themselves. The bottom line is that no matter how bad your situation is now, you have the power to do something about it and change your life.

When I was homeless, I felt like giving up many times, but I knew about the power of choice. So, I decided to improve myself and learn as much about myself as I could. I would spend lots of time at the library reading self-development books. The two books that really impacted me were *The Magic* by Ronda Byrne and *The Man's Search for Meaning* by Victor E.Frankl.

The first one helped me focus on gratitude every day. It may sound cliché for many people, but it really worked for me. So, I was grateful if I could find some shelter, grateful I could see and read, and thankful I was young, strong, and could try and look for work, despite my situation. I knew it was temporary and that it all happened for me, to help me become a better person and improve my mindset. I stopped taking things for granted! I also learned that whenever I focus on gratitude, most negative thoughts would just evaporate from my mind. So, I began practicing my gratitude muscle.

The second book, *The Man's Search for Meaning*, made me go through a profound spiritual awakening. I still have this book on Audible and re-listen to it whenever my mindset slips away and I need to gain perspective. In case you've never heard of it, it's a book written by an Austrian psychiatrist and Holocaust survivor. In his book, he shares what was going on in his mind during the several years he spent in Nazi concentration camps and how he was presecuted as a Jew.

As I was reading his book for the first time, I realized that even though I was homeless, I still had my freedom and I could choose to change my life. I realized I was safe and taken care of. I developed some weird sense of inner peace and tranquility.

Okay, to continue with my story without making it into a biography book . . .

I kept looking for work and experienced many rejections. One day, I met a couple who offered me a room and a job at their restaurant.

To this day, I'm grateful for them and the opportunity they gave me. I also have this deep belief that after hundreds of rejections (who would want to hire a homeless person?), eventually, there is a success. Giving up is a choice you can make, but you can also choose to keep going to gain perspective and grow your mental muscles.

So, I began working a minimum wage job, feeling grateful, and rebuilding myself and my life with a new mindset. I knew that I could learn new things if I wanted to, and that information could be found very inexpensively or even for free, if one was really committed to learning, growing, and improving themselves.

So, I kept working at the restaurant, sometimes even twelve hours a day, and I began studying digital marketing in my free time. I found a YouTube channel by a guy named Miles Beckler. At the time, it was still a small channel dedicated to online business and marketing. I felt like his mindset was very similar to mine and I immediately felt connected to his story. I watched his videos and began taking action on all of them. For example, when he said, "Hey, start reading books on copywriting," I went to the library or got some on Kindle. I didn't cherry-pick, I just followed what he was saying on his channel and focused on learning as much as I could.

I already gave you my number one tip at the beginning of this book, and it was to learn who you truly are and be authentic. Now, the second piece of advice I can give you is to find something you are passionate about or curious about and commit to learning. If you really enjoy the process of learning, you will succeed!

Eventually, I began offering different freelance services in the digital marketing space and making a side income, which ultimately led to a full-time income.

For a while, I kept working two jobs - the restaurant job and my own side business. Eventually, I decided to quit working at the restaurant, found my own place, and began working on my projects full-time. Even though I was still on a very low income, I was so happy because I knew I had the power to change my life. My first clients were the couple that offered me a job and a room at their restaurant. I wanted to give back and use my digital marketing skills to help them gain more clients.

It felt really good to be able to help them. Good karma!

So, from there, I embraced full-time self-employment with all its ups and downs. I began setting goals and achieving them. The first year in my business, I surpassed my goals. The second year, I made double the revenue I wanted to make. And then, in the third year, I didn't achieve my goals! Not only that, but my income was shrinking, and no matter how many new strategies I learned, I could not reach my goals. I felt so scared that I'd lose it all.

I began to ask myself questions to dive deeper. I wanted to know why I didn't achieve my goals. I mean, I was so confident, so sure, because my first ventures had done pretty well—and then what?

Very quickly, I realized it was my mindset, motivation, habits, discipline, and many other things that needed fixing. The problem was internal, not external. Many times, I knew how to grow, but I would sabotage my success, or do the wrong things, or not do anything.

So, this is my story and how I came up with this book! I'm very grateful for the people who helped me and believed in me when I needed help and guidance, and writing this book is my way of giving back to you!

Step #1 Realize Why You Don't Achieve Your Goals in the Desired Timeline

This is the question I asked myself after failing in my third year in business. It was painful! After my initial success and excitement, I ended up moving backwards with no idea how to fix my past mistakes.

As I got deep into self-reflection, I realized I had to reverse-engineer what worked for me previously and get rid of things that were blocking my success, which is exactly how the formula I share in this book was born. I also quickly realized that lack of success is usually something way more profound than motivation.

You see, many people blame the lack of motivation, but I quickly realized it's much deeper than that. What makes us fail is the lack of obsession!

Healthy obsession feels like we are not separate from our goals, but are a part of them.

So, what is the perfect formula for creating a massive obsession? And why do so many people get it wrong (I know I did)?

- 5% of success is inspiration
- 5% of success is motivation
- 90% of success is commitment

Please note that nothing is set in stone; this is how I see it, and this is what works for me. If someone thinks they need a bit more inspiration, that's okay. They're an adult, and they know what's best for them.

However, in my experience, inspiration and motivation are only a small percentage of your success.

And as a high achiever, you want to achieve, right? So many people chase motivation, and when I ask them what they need it for, they have no clue.

My guess is that they're seeking energy or life force. They just feel tired of life, or their physical energy is very low for some reason.

If that's your case, and your physical and mental energy is very low, I recommend you seek medical advice first to check your overall health. Perhaps you're lacking some nutrients or experiencing some health issue. Maybe you're allergic to something. Who knows? But a self-help book will not help here, and you might need professional health or medical advice to fix your low energy problem.

On the other hand, some people think they need motivation, but the real problem is that they feel deeply depressed or traumatized, and should also seek professional help first. So, if you have trouble getting out of bed or doing simple tasks, this can be a mental health problem, not a motivation problem, so seek professional advice if that's the case.

My third piece of advice, even before we get into the meat and potatoes of this book, is to prioritize your health and do frequent check-ups. What you perceive as low motivation may actually be low health. As a high achiever, you want to think like a high performer and take care of your health first. So simple, but most people overlook it. Prevention can be the best cure!

Yet, somehow, so many people get misled into thinking that they just need more motivation, whereas the root of their problem and the true remedy to solve it can be something completely different (and will not be found in a motivational book).

With that being said, let's have a look at our formula again:

- 5% of success is an inspiration
- 5% of success is motivation
- 90% of success is the commitment

An example from my early success story is how I got inspired when I discovered the world of digital marketing and people who were successful with it.

That inspiration gave me my "why" and a vision for life (a location-independent online business I can run from anywhere in the world). That got me started.

Then, there was my immediate motivation: being able to get my own place and do this online thing full-time; being able to live life on my terms.

Finally, there was a commitment—and this is what most people struggle with. Why was I committed? Well, I wanted to gain skills and learn digital marketing. So, I was okay with failing along the way. I knew it would be part of the journey.

However, most of the people I began my digital marketing journey with missed that part. They got inspired and felt motivated, but lost their fire as it got harder. They quit because they wanted immediate results and didn't understand the law of commitment.

Another example—health and fitness. Most people get excited looking at some models on Instagram and a new diet that can help them lose weight. They get started and then give up because they can't see fast results (well, years of eating fast food and not exercising might need more than a few days of on-and-off dieting).

Most people don't think that way; they imagine immediate results and simply hate getting committed to the process. Now, I know how it feels, because I've been there too. I can't even tell you how many schemes or fad diets I'd bought.

It was only when I realized that it's the process and committing to it that can set me free that my life began to change.

Unfortunately, after experiencing some initial success, I stopped doing the inner work and took things for granted. I lost my inspiration, motivation, and commitment. I was no longer obsessed, I was complacent and in a very bitter mindset, and this is precisely why my third year in business wasn't a success. Once again, I had to go back and reverse-engineer what had worked for me previously, and I quickly discovered that this is how all successful people operate. They never trade healthy obsession and commitment for complacency and lack of vision.

So, stay committed like your life depends on it - because it does!

Let's analyze inspiration, motivation, and commitment again.

And yes, you'll need your notebook now to do some self-reflection work.

Your Inspiration

Inspiration is the reason why you started. It's also your vision. For example, you want to start a business to enjoy financial freedom and live a nice lifestyle to take care of your family. Or you want to be healthy, look good, be able to play with your kids and grandkids, and enjoy more energy.

Your Motivation

Motivation is your immediate aim, or in other words, your short-term why. For example, you want to pay the bills or fit in those jeans again. Or you want to look a certain way when you go to the beach. You can also motivate yourself on demand by setting short milestones for yourself and staying accountable.

For example, I have a fitness accountability buddy, and he knows my workout plan and makes sure I stick to it. If I don't, I have to give him fifty bucks. I do the same for him! After sticking to our workout plans for the entire week, we reward ourselves by having a nice meal out. Works well for me! This is how I get my immediate motivation on demand to take action. Using this strategy, I'm getting used to my new fitness habit, and it's becoming second nature to me. I have an accountability buddy because I know that I tend to put off my workouts, or find some excuses like, "oh I have lots of work to do." I also know that when I stick to my workout plan, I feel more energized and do a better job with my businesses.

Question:

Ask yourself what your weakness is (I just told you mine!). What do you usually postpone by looking for excuses? Can you get some accountability to be able to push through and take immediate action? Do it, then find an accountability partner. Yes, I know it's nothing new and you've heard it before, good for you. Now, be sure to apply it! Perhaps you struggle with getting up early? Or going to bed early? Or making a salad instead of binging on fries?

It's always those little things that can make a difference and influence your health, life, family, and career goals!

Finally, both inspiration and motivation are useless if there is no long-term commitment to something bigger. It's the commitment that gets you the visible results, such as a bank account filled with money, a steady client base, or a healthy body.

And here's the sad truth to understand: the world doesn't care about your short-term motivation or inspiration, it only cares about the long-term commitment that leads to tangible results.

People often tell me, "I'm committed, yet I still fail!"

I tell them, "Well, if you're truly committed and the goal you're working toward is genuinely yours, keep failing. There's nothing wrong with that, it's all a part of the process."

When you're truly committed, you don't complain. Instead, you try to fix your mistakes and improve your mindset, strategy, or any other obstacle on your journey.

So, when someone tells me they are committed yet they fail, I know they're asking the wrong question. The right question should be: *I'm now working on this goal to get this result, and I'm looking for ways to improve my process. Here's what's not working, here's what's working, here's all the data to analyze. Is there anything I can improve?*

If you're really committed to the process, you're also committed to learning and hiring true experts or learning from them. Once again, there is no such thing as a lack of money or time. You can always find both. Even if you're really broke, or homeless like I was, you can find time to research all the information you need for free or very inexpensively. It's all about your inner resourcefulness.

This is what commitment is!

And in my experience, the more pain we feel, the more committed we are. This is why I failed in my third year of business. I was already comfortable and I began complaining, criticizing everyone around me, and thinking I was the best and there was no need to improve.

That affected my commitment, my actions, and eventually, my motivation and inspiration. So, I had to start all over again and set bigger goals for myself so that I could leave my comfort zone and experience a little bit of motivational pain.

The reason why I'm telling you this is so that you can hopefully avoid my mistakes because, trust me, they can be very costly - not only in terms of dollars lost but also your health, wellbeing, and even your personal relationships and happiness.

Now, before we get into our exercises, remember:

There's a big difference between wanting and practicing!

Gurus say you can be whatever you want. Kindly, I disagree!

I say you don't always get what you want, but you almost always get what you practice!

Wanting alone is just the first step, and needless to say, you need to know exactly what you want. This is the journey of self-discovery. But then there is practice, which is not sexy for most people!

Most people get inspired and excited. They get some business or self-help book or a program, then log into the Facebook group that comes with it and ambitiously post their goals and what they want.

But they never commit; they never practice. Then, they blame lack of motivation, passion, or talent.

Well, yeah, I think it's pretty obvious that some people are more cut out for certain things. We should always align our goals and actions with our natural passions, motivations, and talents. However, even if you're super talented at something, naturally gifted, or you have a passion for it, you gotta keep practicing.

For example, I love writing; I'm passionate about it. In the past, I've written lots of content for different websites (mostly for Search Engine Optimization purposes). So, having the goal of writing this book aligns with my natural passion and motivation, but I still learn and practice. I read books on how to write better and how to connect with readers. I hire expert editors and proofreaders who can help me write better and I get their feedback.

I don't want you to think this book is now like some other self-help book where you just write your goals. It's just the first step! Then, you must commit to non-stop, relentless repetiton and practice. And this is when it can get a bit tough, but I'm sure you can do this!

So, let's go through the process, step by step.

Questions and Exercises:

1.What's your inspiration? Your big "why" and your big vision?

2.Why did you start doing what you're doing, or why do you want to get started?

3.What exactly do you want, and what do you want your life to look like?

4.Where do you want to live? What car do you want to drive? What about your ideal day?

5.What are your purely materialistic goals? Write as many as you can. How do they make you feel?

6.What are your spiritual goals? Is there a "why" bigger than you and your materialistic goals? If yes, write it down. If not, don't worry - if it comes, it comes. If it doesn't, there is nothing wrong with having only materialistic goals for the time being. As you progress on your journey and discover something bigger, add it to your list and redo this exercise.

One of the mistakes I often see people make (especially young people) is that they get too stuck on their spiritual or deeper purpose or life path.

I was there too; I get it. But trust me, eventually it will come. So, for now, focus on staying in motion and testing different options.

Usually, purpose and the big spiritual "why" come to people who have tried different things in life and even failed at some of them. Nothing wrong with that!

For now, go with something that makes you excited, that gives you a natural high and makes you feel good and positive.

Use that image in your mind whenever you feel like crap!

For example, if your inspiration is to become a revolutionary high-end coach working with high-level clients, be sure to create an exciting vision around it. Design your ideal day in your mind. Think about which aspects of your day make you feel good.

Because later, when you face rejection or don't manage to sign as many clients as you want, you start feeling like crap.

When that happens, just focus your mind on your vision again.

It seems simple, but it works. Yet, very few people do it!

One of my first online businesses was in affiliate marketing. In case you don't know what it is, it's a bit like being an online salesman. You promote products other people created with your referral links, and when someone buys, you get a commission.

So, to do that business successfully, I had to learn different aspects of digital marketing, such as SEO, blogging, and some paid traffic.

The first few months were very frustrating; I had so much to learn and nothing to show for it. In those moments of frustration and having to do the same thing all over again, without even knowing if it would work, I would imagine my affiliate dashboard. I would visualize the money I made and how I felt. And yeah, I know it's materialistic. And sounds woo woo too. Still, it helped me keep taking action when I was still making zero.

The bottom line is to build a simple mental image around whatever you find inspiring. Perhaps your "why" is that you want to travel the world. Well, you can imagine being on a plane and feeling the excitement or hanging out on a beautiful beach with a partner of your dreams.

This is what gets you started!

Now, you need immediate motivation - your small "why" and your first milestone. Perhaps you want to get out of debt, pay off your mortgage faster, invite your spouse to a nice holiday, or get some nice clothes. Or perhaps you simply want to be able to pay your bills without any pressure?

Write it all down!

- Now, have a look at your inspiration and ask yourself, what realistically can you achieve in the next twelve months?
- How realistic is your answer on a scale of one to ten?

If you think it's less than five, ask yourself why.

You already know there is no such thing as blaming other people and circumstances. Just acknowledge why you think it's not that realistic, then think of what you can do to make it more realistic soon!

If you gave it more than five, it means you think it's pretty realistic for you to get a good portion (or even all) of your vision in the next twelve months. You feel pretty comfortable about it, so ask yourself:

- Can you raise the bar? Would that motivate you to achieve your goal faster? Could a higher goal help you stay more motivated or efficient?
- Finally, how committed are you?

If I told you that you will not see any results in three months but would be successful after that, would you still commit to taking action?

And if I told you that you will not get any results for six months, even though you give it your all, would you still commit?

And what if I told you that there is no guarantee?

So, you may end up working hard and not getting any results for a long time, or having to start from scratch.

This is where it gets a bit ugly, but it's also very liberating because it will help you work on the right goals.

Remember when I told you how difficult it was for me to earn money with digital marketing? At first, I didn't get any results and I didn't make any money.

But I was okay with it because I knew I was learning transferrable and marketable skills that could always be monetized in one way or another if I kept working hard.

This is why I'm a big believer in alignment—working on the right things and things that you enjoy doing anyway. So, even if you don't get any results or it takes longer than you expect, you feel peaceful and liberated in knowing you'll always be able to take what you've learned and use it for something else.

For example, maybe your goal for the next six months is to lose a ton of weight. But six months pass, and even though you did lose some weight, it wasn't as much as you wanted, even though you began to eat healthily and hit the gym.

You can see this as a failure or success. I would see it as a success, because even though you still didn't lose as much weight as you wanted, you're a better, healthier, and more disciplined person.

Perhaps you'll realize you don't need to lose all that weight to love yourself and be happy, and you will take pride in the fact that now you're improving your health, which is great for your long-term wellbeing.

It's all about finding joy in the process!

Also, by taking action and staying committed, you'll be more likely to know what works for you and what doesn't. So much better than a person who buys zillions of fad diet books and never uses any of them.

Or let's say you want to get a better position at your company. You spend a year learning new skills and investing in yourself, but someone else still gets that promotion. Well, it may suck at first, especially if you feel like the person chosen is not as qualified as you.

So, what would you do? Would you complain about it or just move on and embrace the fact that now you're more qualified, even if management didn't take notice?

What you learn in the process of taking action and staying committed is something that becomes the new you. So, even if you don't achieve your goals right away, you've already moved forward and are much closer to them. Next time, it will be easier, so don't give up.

The only reason to give up is when you realize you've been working on a goal that wasn't actually your goal, but someone else's goal. That can be very liberating too! Why stick to something you're not even passionate about long-term? So, yeah, in some cases, it makes sense to quit!

For example, a good friend of mine was a successful online fitness influencer for a few years. She received lots of appreciation for her work and made a great living. Many people envied the success she created for herself. But one day, she told me she wasn't passionate about her work anymore and she lost her patience. She told me it was a struggle for her to get out of bed and create the same content all over again, trying to motivate people to eat healthy and work out.

But she kept going, because her business was already doing well and she felt like it was expected of her.

So, we dove a little deeper, and it turned out she was more passionate about business and marketing than she was about being an influencer. As she grew her brand, she became very passionate about marketing (and very good at it) and felt like she could add more value and impact the world in a bigger way by helping other businesses grow.

The solution? It's all about being true to yourself and following your passion.

One day, my friend decided to quit her fitness business and told her followers she would stop creating new content as she moved on to something else. Then, she created her marketing consulting business, and she loves it. It's all about the courage to say no and move on if needed.

The bottom line is that one thing can lead you to the next. If you think it's time to quit and do something else, don't spend too much time dwelling on it. Better focus on at least testing your new idea or

Plan B. Also, you want to work on your true goals and dreams to create the life and career you want. You don't want to build something you're not passionate about in the long run.

More on True Commitment

Let's say you want to improve your social skills and get better at talking to women (or men).

You read books, you learn, you go out and practice, and yet you still experience rejection. Once again, you have a choice. Maybe you will give up and label yourself as shy. Or perhaps you will come to the conclusion that it's better for you to be yourself and listen to your instincts and just socialize more, honestly and authentically, without trying to be someone else or impress people with some lines or things you're supposed to say to get attention.

Isn't that liberating?

You don't fail; you succeed or you learn. You practice for the bigger show!

Perhaps you want to start a new business. You got a program from a legitimate, successful expert; you are learning and taking action. And yet, you don't hit your goals.

Once again, even though it takes longer, you're now a much better and more disciplined person. You have a better mindset and skillset. So, the next time you attempt a new business, it will be easier.

As you take action and stay committed, you gain more knowledge about yourself and more clarity about what you want. Taking action and enjoying the process is the best thing you can do to get accurate data about yourself.

Sometimes, you may even decide to change the goal, and that's fine too. Like I said, if you feel like the goal is not for you, then move on to something else. However, I can almost guarantee that any skill or positive mindset shift you gain by taking action and staying in the trenches will eventually serve you for years to come.

Ask yourself: now that there's no such thing as failing, how does it feel? Isn't that liberating? And doesn't it feel good to dream big, want big, and practice big?

Step #2 Why Waiting for Unlimited Motivation Can Be a Trap and What You Should Focus on Instead

As I was writing this book, an interesting thing happened - and it happened at just the right time!

You see, when I got started on writing this book, I just sat down and wrote over six thousand words without any breaks. I had an outline to stick to and was so excited. So, I started writing this book with a huge win! As I stopped, I had an ambitious plan to repeat the process the following day and just keep moving forward according to the outline until the book was finished.

Seven days later, I was purposely distracting myself with other things - anything but writing! So, why am I telling you this? Shouldn't I try hard to position myself as some perfect and infallible guru? Or an unbeatable authority on the topic of human motivation? Someone who always gets things done, no matter what, so that I'm more credible or so that you follow me?

Actually, I don't care. Instead, I prefer to tell you what's going on behind the scenes as I'm working on this book! Getting off track for several days gave me a few interesting things to share.

So, instead of being an infallible and perfect guru who always gets everything right, I believe I can help you more by being authentic.

As one of my mentors used to say, there are gurus and do-rus. Gurus put in a ton of effort to convey a certain image—the image of an indestructible and perfect authority, while do-rus focus on authentically sharing what's really going on behind the scenes.

Honest and authentic authority is created by teaching and sharing the truth. Gurus talk, do-rus do.

So, this section of the book is not something I wrote in my book outline. It just happened.

I left this book for a week, even though my original plan was to work on it every day. I started super pumped and my first writing session went extremely well, but then I began putting things off. Instead of following through, I spent the next six days focusing on other projects.

This is something that can happen to you as well, and if you think that motivation comes and goes and we can succeed only when we're super pumped and motivated, you may end up moving away from your vision and goals.

Grow Your Motivation Muscle

What got me back on track was the concept of the motivation muscle. And this is something that was a part of the outline. As someone who used this concept before, I have different reminders all around my office and apartment, such as cards. One of them says: *everything is a muscle, and motivation is a muscle too!*

This is how I think about motivation. So, even though I got off track for several days, I'm back on it now. And you can always get back on track too, whenever you want. The more you wait with something, the harder it becomes.

Several years ago, I'd just label myself as motivated or not motivated. If I just stopped working on a project, I would blindly accept it as losing my motivation, so I'd wait for a better moment.

The problem is that tomorrow never comes! All you have to start changing your life is the NOW - the present moment.

Motivation is a muscle, and the sooner you accept this concept, the better. It will help you push through, so even if you get off track, you can always get up, brush yourself off, and start taking massive action again.

Getting started is one thing, but then we need to keep going. Most motivational books only talk about the first step, taking action, which is great. Very few focus on what's going on behind the scenes as we take the first steps and face our fears, doubts, and inner demons.

In my case, I wrote the first part of this book and I just freaked out. A part of me got scared, and I began asking myself negative questions. *What if someone from my family reads it and they don't like it? What if I can't convey my message through this book and I'll come across as another motivational guru?*

In other words, my mind got filled with negative questions. And so, I kept myself busy doing other things and justifying my actions by saying, "Oh, well, if I do those things now, then I can switch off and just finish this book."

Finally, after a few days, I realized what was going on in my mind and decided to ask myself better questions. I believe that our mind works like a search engine, so we might as well use it to ask good, empowering questions. Instead of asking myself questions like "What if I write this book and people don't like it?" I began asking myself "What if I write this book and people like it?"

I rewrote all negative questions into positive ones.

This is the first step to working on your motivation muscle. It's all about non-judgmental awareness of negative self-talk.

Then, you change those questions into positive ones.

And finally, you take advantage of that positive mental momentum and you get back to working on your project. Don't beat yourself up for getting off track, just get back on it. Most people don't have the courage to get up and brush themselves off, but you are different. Now, you understand how it works.

Another interesting thing is that as I'm working on this book again, I feel more and more motivated and energized. I dove deeper, acknowledged what was going on, refused to allow any negative voices to spoil my efforts, and made a decision to finish what I was working on.

I want you to be very mindful that these things happen and that motivation is not a linear process. Working on your motivation muscle is like taking a shower or brushing your teeth; it's something you just must do. The mental part of working on that muscle is becoming aware of the negative voices in your head and rewriting them to your advantage. Then, you must get back on track. This is how you grow your motivation muscle and become truly unstoppable.

There are different definitions of motivation, and I'd encourage you to come up with your own - something that empowers you long-term.

I define motivation as *something that helps you take action now, in this moment.*

You see, there's always something trying to bring us down, both internally (negative voices in our heads) and externally (stressors, people, environment).

People who seem to be unstoppable and achieve their goals faster know how to focus, say no, and set incredible boundaries. This is why their motivation muscle is stronger. They take action to get rid of internal and external distractions, which allows them to stay motivated.

Motivation is not something that just comes! And if you want to be successful, you can't depend on waiting for motivation; you need to work on it and grow it by working on yourself and your mindset.

Here's the truth that most people don't want to hear, but I know you're different:

Dedicating yourself to repetitive work, even when you don't feel like it or some negative voice in your head tells you to stop, is not easy!

However, it helps you build your motivation muscle and become a stronger human being.

So, here's a simple exercise that will help you work on your motivation muscle:

- What helps you achieve your goals?

Examples:

- actions you take, your schedule, the way you talk to yourself, books you read or coaches you hire, people you hang out with, foods you eat, your environment

Now, ask yourself:

- What prevents you from achieving your goals?

Examples:

- Avoiding sales calls or creating content, getting up late, binging on Netflix, watching YouTube videos, scrolling on social media, getting caught up in gossip and drama, eating crappy foods, etc.

Take your time to do this exercise and be honest with yourself. We often kill our motivation by spending too much time doing things that take us away from our goals.

People always ask me how to stay motivated, productive, inspired, and disciplined. The answer is very simple: embrace the investor mindset.

Whatever actions you take today, ask yourself if you're investing in your long-term success or not?

Once again, be honest with yourself and go through this exercise several times. Your answers will depend on your vision and your values. Everyone is different. The simple rule of thumb is to lessen the things that do not align with your investor mindset and start adding actions that fuel your goals. This is how you stay motivated. There is no magic pill or magic technique. It's a fusion of different mindsets and actions repeated all over again. Yeah, I know - not very sexy!

Most people love the initial excitement that comes with buying and reading a new self-help book. But diving deeper and facing your inner demons is not always easy!

We should be grateful for that, because it's by doing the things that aren't easy that we build our motivational muscle. Eventually, hard stuff becomes easy and automatic.

For example, I know many fiction authors who write full time, and many of them can quickly crank out five thousand words a day, nearly every day. They don't even think about it, they just do it - it's a part of who they are.

They don't talk about what they're going to write and they don't hang out online talking about how cool they are. They just stay behind the scenes and write. Most of them told me they just get up, grab a cup of coffee, write their daily word count, and then move on with the rest of the day. A pretty simple, action-focused plan, right?

Successful YouTubers publish daily videos. It's just what they do. Creating videos is a part of who they are. I remember watching a video by Aaron Doughty (he has a successful YouTube channel in the spirituality niche) where he shared how he transitioned from working a job he didn't enjoy to making a good living from his passion. The answer is simple: he focused on making daily videos and embraced his new self-image of being a full-time content creator.

Whatever it is that you want to do, you always have a choice: you can be a wannabe or a pro. Pros do what they're supposed to do and grow their motivation muscle by overcoming the negative voices in their heads and taking consistent actions, even when things get tough.

Remember, we don't always get what we want, but we always get what we practice!

You think like a pro, and you're serious about your goals and vision for life. So, have a look at the *Grow Your Motivation Muscle Exercise* and the things you need to either do more or let go of.

Be sure to design your week accordingly and stick to your schedule. It's as simple as that; there's no big philosophy behind it.

Avoid the enemies that kill your motivation, internally and externally.

Yes, sometimes things happen and you might get off track like I did. At first, it seems innocent, doesn't it? Like skipping the gym a couple of times.

You may tell yourself, *Oh, well, if I skip the gym a couple of times, it's not like I will put on weight immediately.*

Or, *If I take a day off from creating content to grow my business, it's not that I will go bankrupt.* And yeah, it's true.

If you skip something once or twice as a big exception, nothing happens at first. You don't see any negative results, so you may be tempted to do more "cheat days." And eventually, what happens?

If you keep skipping the gym, you may eventually start putting on weight. And then it's harder, because you feel like you have to start all over again and you need much more energy. Not only that, but since all areas of life are interconnected, by neglecting your health, you may also end up hurting your overall energy and wellbeing, which can reverberate on your professional life.

If you keep skipping important activities in your business, your competitors may eventually take over, and you may start losing your clients.

The bottom line is that how you do one thing is how you do everything.

You need a smart plan to follow, a plan that will not burn you out. For example, when I started working on this book, I started very big and cranked out six thousand words on day one. Then, I felt mentally tired and was more prone to the negativity in my head and escaping to excuses and procrastination.

It's actually one of my weak points; I often take too much action and then burn myself out. I'm very aware of this, and I'm working on it. Yes, overdoing things can be as bad as not doing enough.

So, as soon as I catch myself in this "over high achiever mindset," I remind myself to develop a plan that allows me to be consistent without burning myself out. I can't afford to risk a burnout because these usually make me stop taking action.

I redesigned my week, and I write no more than one or two thousand words a day. If any ideas come, I just write them down in my Evernote app.

Some people take too much action all at once and burn themselves out. Other people may be going too slow. Both approaches can be detrimental. Once again, be honest with yourself and experiment with different schedules to see what works for you and what allows your motivation muscle to grow.

Scheduling a gym or any physical activity is an excellent way to grow your motivation and discipline muscle. It's also a great way to help you embrace long-term thinking and avoid instant gratification. And this is such a great mindset for any ambitious individual to cultivate!

If you haven't done the *Grow Your Motivation Muscle Exercise* from this section, please do yourself a favor and do it now. Don't postpone it, because if you do, it will only get harder. Break any vicious cycle now, by taking action and getting honest with yourself.

This exercise will help you become truly committed to your vision and see things as they really are, instead of just wishing they were better.

Find joy and meaning in this process, because even if it takes longer to achieve your goals, your motivation muscle will get stronger and it will be much easier for you next time. You will be a different person, with a new, transformed mindset, and your actions (and your reality) will start to reflect that.

In the next step, we're going to focus on commitment, focus, and avoiding distractions.

Step #3 What Most Motivational Books Miss—Your Commitment Muscle

Commitment can be learned and mastered, just like your motivational muscle can be grown if your goal is truly yours and you're passionate about it.

Speaking of passion, most people don't know that the word "passion" comes from the Latin word "passio", which means "suffering." And no, I'm not implying you must become a martyr and torture yourself to achieve your goals. I'm saying you must accept the pain that usually comes with any attempt to follow your passion.

Nowadays, however, most people use the word "passion" as if it was some magic pill that will give the wings to do incredible things without even having to think about it.

Let me tell you this: Yes, passion can give you wings to do incredible things. For me, personally, if you are passionate about something, it means you really want it. And because you want it, you're willing to practice it.

Once again, we don't always get what we want, but we almost always get what we practice!

Passion and commitment go hand in hand. When you commit to something, it means you also understand that there might be some suffering and bad days involved, and you will still stay committed and push through. This is how the most significant breakthrough comes. For example, when I started my affiliate business, I felt like quitting so many times. It felt so frustrating to do all this work, invest in different tools and softwares, and still have nothing to show for it. Yet, I pushed through, and let me tell you this: There's always the light at the end of the tunnel. I was tempted to quit or look for some new, shiny object.

But then I remembered what I learned about passion and the real meaning behind it, and I asked myself if I was willing to suffer for it.

Then, I thought about my grandparents and great-grandparents and how hard they had it during the Second World War in Nazi-occupied Europe. The constant fear for the lives of themselves and their families. The pain after losing a loved one. Hunger. Feeling powerless. That was their reality!

And there I was, sitting in my safe apartment, working on my laptop and complaining that it took too long for me to make money. So, that gave me some perspective about real suffering. The truth is, we often exaggerate and make mountains out of molehills.

Think about your ancestors and their problems. Then, ask yourself again, what are you really complaining about?

So, here's what you need to do to master your commitment - and trust me, it will serve you well in all areas of your life. People will automatically think of you as a reliable person and want to do business with you, because they will see that you always keep your word and do what you said you would.

The first step you need to take is to release any expectations of achieving things fast. I'm not saying you should remove your ambition to succeed big, just don't think of it as an event or something that is supposed to happen quickly.

In this fast-paced Internet and social media world, we often seek instant gratification. We don't even think about the consequences. Unfortunately, we can often see them in our motivation and commitment—or the lack thereof.

Even when I was writing this book, I had to keep releasing many unrealistic expectations. You see, I started off thinking it would be much easier because I had some experience writing blogs. But writing a book is a different story. I immediately caught myself with many negative voices in my head. The more I focused on that negativity, the more reasons I could find to quit or postpone this project.

But then, once again, I reminded myself to release all those expectations and ask myself where I got them from.

As I was researching how to write a book, I came across many pieces of training created by full-time authors, and all they do is write. They have been doing it for many years, so their writing muscle is strong. I learned a lot of useful tips and I'm very grateful for all of them.

However, the theory may be different than practice, and everyone is different. When you do something for the first time, there will always be more obstacles to conquer, even if you prepare yourself by reading books and taking courses or mentorship.

So, I immediately released all the previous expectations I had, one of them being that I could write this book in two weeks - which I clearly couldn't. I simply accepted the fact that it would take longer, and I was okay with that.

I reminded myself of what I learned from the book *The Millionaire Fastlane* by MJ de Marco. Even though the title may seem a bit cheesy or like a get-rich-quick scheme, it's exactly the opposite. In the book, the author, a self-made millionaire, talks about the process versus the event. Whenever someone achieves success - whether it's in business, sports, art, or something else - people only see the tip of the iceberg and immediately assume it was an event.

Oh yeah, he succeeded because he got lucky or someone helped him.

However, there is a whole process of blood, sweat, and tears that most people don't see. Even if they learn about what really went on behind the scenes, they don't want to accept it as their path to success. They always want to get shortcuts or, as MJ de Marco calls it, become a hitchhiker!

What I would add to the concept of process and event is that you need to shift your mindset from *he succeeded because he had it so easy* to *he succeeded despite the fact that there were so many obstacles.*

The sad truth is that when you succeed, you will come across many naysayers who will try to belittle you and your success. They will always try to justify your success to make themselves feel better.

Some people even said I succeeded with my affiliate business because I must have had a top-notch college education in business and marketing, which is not true because I am self-taught.

Ask yourself what kind of person you are. Will you look for excuses and justify why you can't do something? Or will you succeed despite not being born lucky, rich, and successful?

Isn't it ironic that most successful people we read about succeeded even though their initial situation wasn't perfect?

Exercise:

Write down all the obstacles that you think are stopping you from staying committed to your goals. For example:

- I don't have a big capital
- My family is not rich or influential
- I have no experience in business
- English is not my native language
- I am not a quick learner
- I'm too fat or too skinny
- I am dyslexic
- I have ADD
- I'm not disciplined
- Nobody in my family eats healthy, so I can't do it either

What story do you keep telling yourself? Is it:

*I can't succeed with this business opportunity **because** I have no experience in business, and I'm a slow learner.*

Or, is it:

Despite being a slow learner and not having any experience in business, I know I can still succeed with this business opportunity if I work hard at it, stay committed, and enjoy the process. Even if I don't succeed fast, I'm committed because I know that if I keep going, I'll eventually gain knowledge and experience to make it all easier.

What do you choose, excuses or commitment?

I used to look for excuses like, "I'm not a good enough writer to write a book. I'm not a self-help guru, so who am I to write a book on motivation? Why would anyone want to read it?"

I gave myself the chance to dive deeper, get some training, and do research. Then, I came across many successful authors who were not even native speakers of English. They had to work harder and had their unique set of obstacles, but they stayed committed and were rewarded for it.

I still had some negative voices in my head telling me that maybe others could do it because of this and that, but I couldn't. Once again, I caught myself being an "I can't do it because" person and had to rewrite my story to: "Despite being new to all this, I can learn, even if it takes longer."

Remember, what you focus on expands. If you keep focusing on why something is not possible, your mind will keep expanding on all the negative voices telling you why you should quit. However, if you promise yourself to be persistent and focus on how something can be learned or mastered, you will be the creator of your own destiny.

Another thing that will help you stay committed to the process is amplifying a peaceful state while removing any toxicity from your environment.

Do this exercise to determine what around you is toxic and what is peaceful.

Toxic:

Naysayers

Verbally abusive people

Unhealthy foods

Addictions

Disorganized workspace

No fixed schedule

Peaceful:

Practicing gratitude

Celebrating little wins on your journey

The mastermind of like-minded people led by an experienced mentor

High-quality educational trainings

Quality foods

Fixed schedule and success rituals

Ask yourself what you are going to let go of to stay committed to the process. And ask what you are going to add to your routine or environment to help you grow your commitment muscle.

I wish I could promise you that your thoughts will be extremely positive for life, but we both know that life doesn't work that way.

So, be prepared for some negativity going on in your head. Be aware of any negative mindset patterns, but don't beat yourself up over them. Instead, use them as feedback!

Often times, as we put ourselves through challenging tasks way outside our comfort zone, our minds begin to rebel. Sometimes, we may even get reminded of past traumas or some negative memories from childhood or some feelings of unworthiness.

Don't let those feelings stop you. Also, remember that you're not alone. All great thinkers and achievers had to go through similar patterns as they committed to their goals. Never be afraid to reach out for help and talk to someone who understands; it can be a therapist, mentor, or a community of like-minded people. You may think that your circumstances are unique, and maybe they are, but I can almost guarantee that someone has already been through what you're going through, or has a deep understanding of it, and you could benefit from talking to them.

Exercise:

Think about the people who inspire you. It can be someone from your family, friends, church, or someone you follow online.

Find 1-3 people who you admire and respect for their achievements.

Now, research them and find out the real process and commitment behind their success. Did they always have it easy? Did it take them longer?

Most likely, yes!

Take a piece of paper and write this down:

(Name of a person you admire) also struggled on their journey. But now, they (list their success).

If they can do it, then I can do it too!

Whenever you feel down and your commitment muscle is shrinking, ask yourself what the person you admire would do, if they were you.

I'm pretty sure this exercise will help you get unstuck!

Inspiration is not that hard, but you already know it's a small percentage of success. After all, it's not that hard to watch motivational videos and get a bit excited. Unfortunately, motivation, muscle, and commitment are way harder. And this is what most motivational materials don't tell you, because then they would decrease their sales and popularity. After all, most people like what's easy and effortless, especially now, in the area of instant gratification.

However, inspiration does not always equal results, but commitment does.

Working on your commitment also requires working on your focus and eliminating all kinds of distractions. Every action you take has consequences. For example, you may take a break from work and enjoy a cup of tea or coffee and go for a short walk or move your body (outside or in your workspace). It's a simple action that will allow you to stay focused and productive and, therefore, committed.

At the same time, you can also choose to scroll through your Facebook news feed. And it can be innocent; perhaps you just comment on a friend's holiday picture, log out, and get back to work. Or, perhaps you will get distracted and wonder why they're always on holiday and you're not; perhaps their business is better than yours, and maybe your doing something wrong.

Who knows? Perhaps then you will see an ad from the latest get-rich-quick guru who's a pro at fear-based marketing. Immediately, he will appeal to your deepest pains, fears, insecurities, and frustrations. He will get your attention in a few seconds, and with his unique mechanism and copywriting skills, easily convince you that his way of making money is the best and that you're missing out. You will register for a webinar, purchase his products, and play around with it for a few weeks, only to realize it wasn't as easy as he presented it would be.

Well, some may say this is how you learn; sometimes you have to lose money to learn how to think for yourself.

However, in my opinion, there are much more profound consequences than bad investments in products you don't need. There's also lost time, energy, and momentum. Perhaps you were working on something that was very close to being successful, but then you got distracted with some shiny objects and lost your focus for a few weeks. Now, you have to go back to what you were doing before and re-commit. Not only that, but there are all those voices in your head: *Oh, why am I such a loser? Why do I always fall for this stuff? Why do all those gurus have it so easy but I don't?*

Time and energy are the most precious asset we have!

Let's say a person is on a healthy eating plan and slowly losing weight. But then, they get distracted and see an advertisement for some fad diet or pills. They give up their healthy lifestyle to get results fast and end up wasting time and maybe even damaging their health on some miracle supplements.

The bottom line is that the more you commit to something, the more you see that the whole world is against you and your commitment. They try to seduce you into thinking you're doing something wrong and want to give you their shortcuts.

The sad truth is that shortcuts don't work, but true commitment does.

Better safe than sorry! You need to protect yourself from distractions because none of them are innocent. They all come with a heavy price tag, and that price is not only your hard-earned money but also your mental health, focus, and self-worth.

The grass is not greener on the other side.

I'm not telling you what to do. If you're getting value from scrolling on social media, then that's fine. But if you feel like too much exposure to social media is slowing you down and killing your efficiency, productivity, and commitment, do something about it now.

Ask yourself how much time per day you spend on social media.

How much would your life improve you if spent that time doing something else, such as:

- reading and learning new skills
- actively working on your business
- spending quality time with your friends and family
- working out
- planning healthy meals
- working on your personal development or spirituality
- Relaxing and lowering stress

Do what you think is best for you!

Personally, I only check my social media after I'm done working. I also deleted most apps from my phone, so I never get distracted. It works well for me, and now I can honestly tell you that I have more time! Suddenly, writing a book seems more doable, and I no longer find myself complaining that I don't have time to write (even though I run a business and have family obligations).

Efficiency and commitment go hand in hand. You do things that make you either more or less efficient. Now, I'm not saying you should live like a monk and don't have any fun (unless you truly want to live like a monk, and there's nothing wrong with that either).

It all comes down to strategic planning. Schedule fun and what I like to call "controlled distractions." For example, it's better to schedule ten minutes a day of scrolling on Facebook or any social media platform than it is to set a goal of quitting social media and then binge on it and feel bad.

Do what's best for you and your commitment, but think long-term and don't allow short-term distractions to interfere with the best version of yourself.

Also, be sure to set boundaries. These are so important, especially when it comes to dealing with your family and friends.

Once again, defining your schedule helps! When I first got started on self-employment and online work, most of my family members thought I was always available because I was working for myself and didn't have to go to a "real job". I quickly realized it was my fault, because I wasn't setting any boundaries with them, and as a new business owner, my productivity muscle was still pretty weak.

I was always in a very reactive state and didn't have a clearly-defined schedule or boundaries. I was also stupid and naïve enough to keep telling my family how cool running an online business and being my own boss was, without ever talking about any of the negatives. My ego took over, and I just wanted to show everyone how successful I became and that my life was better than everyone else's. So, they thought it was all roses and I had to pay the consequences by living in a reactive state. It was only when I encountered serious problems in my business that I had to readjust my strategy.

So, I told all my friends and family that things had changed for me, and that I had new projects and a new schedule to stick to, and it was pretty much the same as if I was in a normal job. At first, it was hard; I remember my cousin calling me all morning and leaving nasty messages like, "Come on, why are you ignoring me?"

But eventually, they got it, and now everything works well.

If you're self-employed, you might also consider using two phones—one for the family and one for work. Same with social media. I remember using the same profile for everything, and once my mom began commenting on one of my posts about business, it really made me look stupid in the eyes of my clients.

Once again, I take responsibility because I could have prevented it by separating business and family profiles. Also, my mom didn't have any bad intentions, she just saw some post about money, business, and marketing and though it was more like a joke I was posting for friends. Now I'm laughing at it, but back then I was pissed off.

The bottom line is that you should set boundaries with family, friends, colleagues, business partners, and pretty much everyone who enters your life. Some may say you're too disciplined. But eventually, they will love it, because the more boundaries you have and the more disciplined you are, the more peace you can cultivate. In this world of stress and distractions, people are naturally drawn to peaceful people (yeah, I know it sounds bit woo-woo, but try it yourself).

To sum up this section, your commitment is fueled by your peaceful state, and the best way to expand on your peace is by removing distractions and toxicity.

Being organized and committed doesn't mean you can't have fun and be spontaneous. Quite on the contrary! Now that I have my boundaries and stick to my schedule, I finally have the freedom to enjoy most of my evenings and late afternoons off, which helps me cultivate my peace or do things I enjoy doing. Then, I can do a better job at whatever project I'm working on.

This more balanced, boundary-fueled, and organized schedule allows me to enjoy more freedom than when I was being reactive and could never find any time for myself.

You choose!

I hope this chapter gave you something to think about. As always, implement as much as you can, as quickly as you can. It's always those small changes and your commitment to them that gives you the best transformation.

Your Energy and High Performance

To stay committed long-term, you need stamina, health, and energy. All high performers understand that. Why am I mentioning this? Well, not long ago, as I was allowing myself my ten minutes a day to get a bit distracted on social media, I came across a post someone made in a Facebook group dedicated to business and affiliate marketing.

That gentlemen wrote, "I'm so committed to succeeding that now I'm gonna cancel on the gym and exercise routine so that I can hustle more."

And most comments on that post were positive: "Yeah, man! Push it! Go for it! Do it! Hustle hard!"

Now, I am all for hard work and success, but I don't think sacrificing your health is the only way. I'm not a health or fitness expert, so I'm not here to preach to you and tell you how many times a week you should exercise. And if money and business is your priority now, then give it all your focus. But that doesn't mean you should stop working on your health and fitness. Yeah, maybe you can't to go the gym every day. Well, then go twice a week. Or find some free workouts online you can do at home.

Be strategic about your schedule. Personally, I don't think you can succeed at everything at once. There's always one area of life that needs more attention, but they always go together. For example, if you start neglecting your health and fitness, you may eventually start to feel more stressed out or less energized.

When planning your week, be sure to:

- make a list of all distractions and ask yourself how you can avoid them (for example, boundaries with family or blocking some apps on your phone)
- even if your main focus now is work and career, don't sacrifice your health and fitness. Schedule some exercise, and if possible, invest in a nutrition expert to get a balanced meal plan. You will work and concentrate better!

Many people lose motivation simply because they don't have enough energy. Simple tweaks in your weekly schedule, such as adding in two or three workouts and eating healthy meals, can have a significant impact on your other goals. And for hustle lovers, you will hustle better and smarter and more long-term!

For balance lovers—yes, everything is interconnected! And ultimately, health is wealth!

In the next step, we will talk about resilience. Be sure to go through the exercises from this step to make sure your schedule is well planned out.

Step #4 Your No-Complaint Muscle

My definition is simple: Resilience is your no-complaint muscle. The stronger it gets, the more resilient you are. With resilience, you also grow your motivation, dedication, and commitment.

And yes, it's as simple as not complaining!

Now, I'll be the first one to tell you that I used to complain a lot. I could blame my family and my friends because for as long as I can remember, everyone around me would always complain about something.

So, for many years, I lived with a complete lack of awareness, just blindly copying what everyone else was doing- complaining. It was only when I got into self-development and eventually worked with several mindset coaches, a mindfulness expert, and even a therapist that I realized the problem was indeed me and my constant complaining about everything.

It was actually my partner who first told me, "Oh man, you complain a lot. Just listen to yourself! The last half hour, instead of complaining about your advertising cost going up, you could have figured out a better solution!"

Of course, my ego would always come up with an excuse such as, *Oh, come on, I gotta vent out that anger, right?*

And yes, we all deserve to vent out anger, that's for sure, and there is a time for everything. Sometimes, it just makes sense to express our frustrations with a clear intention to find solutions.

So, whenever I'm in a complaining or negative mindset, what I like to do is I allow myself to complain for only a certain amount of time, just to vent it out. Maybe ten minutes, for example. Sometimes, I even write it all down on a piece of paper, then just tear it up and throw it away.

That is how I send signals to my mind: *Okay, stop complaining. You vented out. That's justifiable, but now use your energy for something positive!*

Have you ever noticed that the more you complain, the more excuses you find to avoid taking action?

You can complain about how everyone in your family tends to put on weight easily; it's all genetic, and so, why even bother working out?

Or you may start complaining that all high-level positions at your company are only reserved for people who have contacts, so why even bother applying for promotion?

Oh, and the line of business you want to go in is so competitive, and taxes are getting higher and higher, so why even bother?

Complaints and excuses make us weaker and kill not only our resilience but also our energy, positivity, and overall life force—our ability to move forward, think clearly, and take massive action.

The first step is awareness. Be aware of what is going in your head. If you come to the same realization I came to - that you probably got all that from your family or people you grew up with - be careful not to get in the victim mindset. Take responsibility. Now that you are aware of what is going on, you can choose to transform your mindset and eventually help those around you, too.

When people see you're motivated, happy, and successful, those who are ready for change will get inspired to do so. Of course, some will stay where they are, complaining and belittling your success, but this is a topic for another day, or perhaps even a whole new book.

So, leave all your complaints and excuses at the door. There are people with the same kind of circumstances, or even worse, who still succeed despite what happened to them.

The following exercises will help you grow your resilience muscle:

1. Write down your goals, divided into:

- your financial goals (be very specific in terms of how much money you want to make per month, per year, etc. Have a closer look at your expenses and taxes, so that you can set a specific number that will allow you to live the lifestyle you want.)
- If you work for a company, be sure to set a specific salary you want to receive and the line of work you want to be doing. Think of all the details.
- your life goals, including your health and fitness, your family, etc.

When doing this exercise, be sure to think big because this is the goal of this exercise. The next page will reveal why I want you to think big on this one.

2. Now, what do you think is holding you back from achieving your big dreams?

List all your negative beliefs and feel free to vent them out. Is it your confidence? Competition? Your skills?

Write it all down.

How do those all negative beliefs affect you?

Write them all down on a piece of paper and vent it all out.

3. Now, focus on the positive. Ask yourself what you like about yourself, your skills, and the resources that are available to you.

Focus on gratitude as much as possible. Remember, gratitude removes toxicity and helps you stay committed!

4. Ask yourself how all your beliefs, both positive and negative, can help you. Can you turn negative into positive? Is it really that bad?

Remember, someone always has it worse than you do!

5. Be aware of all kinds of negative triggers. For example, what makes you sad or angry? In my case, talking about my business to my family would always trigger me, because they would often react negatively. So, I just stopped explaining what I do. It's as simple as that! If you get triggered because people ask you too many questions, take their position instead and start asking them what's going on in their life.

Also, remember that you can't control other people and what they do or think, but you can always control your reactions.

This is how you can gradually start erasing your old, negative, or self-conscious mindset. Most people are too absorbed in their own fears and doubts, and not everyone is thinking about you and what you do all the time. Isn't that liberating?

The final exercise is to have a look at all your negative beliefs and rewrite them into positive ones. For example:

"Nobody wants to buy from me" to "I'm great at marketing and selling, it's fun, people love to buy from me and love my products."

"No matter how hard I try I can't lose weight" to "I love moving my body and eating healthy, and I feel better every day! I just love it."

These are just examples to inspire you to create your own affirmations. I even recommend you record yourself saying those positive affirmations and listen to them every day. Trust me, if you can stick to it for a few months, you will notice amazing shifts in the way you think and act.

If you want to skip the affirmation part, let me ask you this—you invested your time, money, and energy into reading this book, so why not get your ROI and follow through?

Make the most of it. How you do one thing is how you do everything. You can do your own affirmations and record them in less than fifteen minutes. It's a great resilience exercise too! Why postpone doing things?

If you could do things faster and act with conviction, how would your life change?

For example, how about filing tax returns as soon as you can and getting it done? How about doing the dishes as soon as you can?

Delayed actions take away from your energy and motivation. If you can do something now, do it now, because this is how you train all your muscles—motivation, commitment, and resilience.

There is someone who had it much worse than you, and still they can get better results. This is what I always say to myself whenever I need a kick in the ass to stop complaining or taking action on something.

Finally, let's start this section with a little bit of reflection.

Why can two people with the same resources, skillset, and background get different results? This is something I got very curious about as I was going through different business courses and programs.

There's nothing too philosophical about it. Yes we could talk about karma or being possessed by some negative energies, but it all comes down to:

- consistency
- your ability to implement what you learn fast
- your ability to ask for honest feedback and not be afraid to take it

- your ability to learn from failure and reframe it into something positive
- your ability to keep taking action, even when you feel scared and things are not going as planned

The good news? You can control all the above factors, and the more you focus on what you can control, the more you grow your resilience muscle!

Never assume that something will not work for you before even trying. You deserve to give yourself a chance and stick to the process. Release your fears of failure, because there is no such thing; you succeed, or you learn.

I can almost guarantee that people who you look up to as successful are successful NOT because of some magic luck or magic set of circumstances, but simply because they failed much more than you did and ultimately learned from their failures.

There is a stupid failure or a smart failure. A stupid failure is when something doesn't go as planned and you choose to make it your identity and haunt you all your life by thinking of yourself as a loser.

A smart failure is when you decide to embrace it and learn as much as you can from it to keep growing your resilience muscle.

Make it your daily mantra- **I don't fail; I succeed, or I learn!**

As weird as it may seem, most people plan for their failure, not for their success. It's because of the fear that they feel. And yeah, I have been there too!

It's pretty much this pattern- you invest in a book, course, or a mentor, and right off the bat, you begin to focus on why it will not work for you and look for all the reasons why other people could become successful or achieve some results but you can't.

Be brutally honest with yourself: Are you planning for your failure or for your success?

What you focus on expands, so choose wisely.

As a person with a strong resilience muscle, promise yourself to focus on responsibility as much as you can!

Let finish this section with a story. A very successful entrepreneur friend of mine has a particular way of teaching responsibility to his kids, which may seem a bit cruel to some people. I'll abstain from judging, because I'm not a parent and know nothing about parenting, I am not saying what he does is right or wrong, I just found it interesting enough to share in this book.

Whenever one of his kids comes to him complaining—for example, "Oh, Dad, my brother took my toy!"—instead of saying, "Oh, poor you," he says, "Well, then why did you leave it on the couch instead of taking it to your room?"

In other words, he wants his kids to be responsible for their actions and sticking to the rules of the household.

Can you apply this to your life too?

Remember when I told you about my family being negative about my business? It really haunted me for a long time and gave me lots of anger and frustration. But then I realized that just like that kid from the story above, I left my toy on a couch instead of taking it to my room.

I didn't set boundaries, and when I first became successful, I was bragging way too much.

Whatever it is that you feel is haunting you or dragging you down, here's my best tip for you:

- Take responsibility
- Try to forgive yourself and others

Commit and repeat!

Do the inner work when needed, because when left undone, it may come back and start haunting you, making you less effective in your endeavors.

Final Words—The 10 Commandments of the Unstoppable Achiever

You now have everything you need to be unstoppable, achieve your goals, and create a better version of yourself.

Whenever you get stuck or you have a terrible day, reread this book, and if needed, redo its exercises.

I'd like to finish this book with my Decalogue of the Unstoppable Achiever, something that can help you push through any obstacle to help you stay motivated and committed to keep moving forward!

Enjoy!

#1 Focus on the legacy and see the bigger picture

Even if you're failing or think you're going too slow, you're creating your story and your legacy. Imagine you're already super successful, and you're talking about your humble beginnings and old struggles to your children or grandchildren.

Suddenly, everything will make sense for you, and you'll be less affected by any obstacles you may encounter.

#2 Ask yourself what you can do now to move forward and stop the cycle of inaction?

Your actions are what the world can see; nobody can see what's in your head. And if you're feeling stuck, chances are you're too in your head. So, focus on something you can do right here and right now!

#3 Instead of asking for privileges and complaining about what you don't have, focus on your responsibilities and what you can control here and now.

True power lies in being responsible for your actions.

#4 Controlling your muscles is easier than controlling your emotions, so focus on growing your motivation muscle.

Take consistent action. Don't rely on feeling good, because feelings come and go. If you only take action when you feel good, it will be hard to stay consistent to reach your goals.

#5 Instead of not taking any action and fearing failure, reframe everything you do into an experiment you are curious about.

You can't fail; you succeed, or you learn! Yes, what you do is important, but don't put too much importance on it. You can let go by seeing whatever it is that you do as some fun experiment you're curious about.

#6 Emotions are just feedback. Don't try to fight them, just observe them and ask yourself what they are trying to tell you.

Even if you feel like crap, you can still choose to stay committed and grow your motivation muscle.

#7 Instead of thinking too much or talking about your goals with people who don't support you, focus your energy on doing instead.

You get what you practice, not what you talk about!

#8 Stop looking for guarantees and don't get too attached to your final outcome.

Instead, focus on enjoying the process, because it's the process that makes you stronger and grows your motivation muscle. Even if you don't reach your goals now, you will grow into an unstoppable human being, and everything will be much easier next time.

#9 Positive thoughts are great, but be sure to back them up with massive positive action.

The law of attraction has the word "action" in it. Focusing on the positive and staying in a peaceful and positive mindset can be great for your mental wellbeing, but be sure to support your positive thoughts with positive actions. Some days, you will have negative thoughts, and the best way to transform them is to take positive action that gets you closer to your goals. Act and grow rich!

#10 Don't treat life so personally, and life will treat you better too!

Don't let the reality that surrounds you control your actions. Instead, use your actions to mold your reality.

You have the power to change your life. Everything is unfolding just like it should.

You can always choose!

Thank you for reading to the very end, and good luck!

Let's Stay in Touch – Mark's Mailing List

I invite You to join my mailing list to receive free instant access to bonus worksheets for self-coaching + daily mindset tips to help you grow your motivation muscle and stay committed to your goals.

No spam, no BS, only useful information and resources to help you become unstoppable!

Sign Up Link:

www.bitly.com/Mark-Email-Newsletter

(when typing this into your browser, please note that this link is case-sensitive)

If you have any questions about this book, or want to say Hi, feel free to email me at:

markerdatbooks@gmail.com

Let Me Help You

Finally, if you have a couple of minutes, I'd really appreciate your honest review on Amazon and other online platforms.

Would be great if you could let me and others know:

-why you got this book

-did you find it helpful ?

-the #1 lesson you learned from it

-how is this book different from (or similar to) other self-help books you've read?

-who, do you think should read this book, who might find it helpful?

Thank You in advance for your time and feedback.

This is my first book, English is my second language, so, I had to put in extra effort and had my own set of obstacles while writing it. Imagine writing a book in a different language, it can be quite a challenge (but so worth it!).

I definitely want to write more books to inspire you on your self-improvement journey. I want to be as helpful as I can and your feedback/reviews offer me the data I need to write better while focusing on the topics you need most help with.

Printed in Great Britain
by Amazon